JOHN BURNINGHAM'S
CHAMPAGNE

"Too much of anything is bad, but too much Champagne is just right."

Mark Twain

JOHN BURNINGHAM'S
CHAMPAGNE

LochAwe Books

*In fondest memory of Rose Foot
whose humour, commitment and
skilful research were crucial to the
creation of this book.*

FOREWORD
by Joanna Lumley

What a stroke of luck it was to be cast as Patsy in *Absolutely Fabulous*, in which my character is routinely described as 'Champagne-swilling'! Not an episode went by without us cracking open a bottle of Bolly, or the Veuve: sometimes, with grotesquely bad taste, mixing up a Stoli-Bolly cocktail and quaffing bubbles from morning to night. True, our on-screen Champagne was only ginger ale: and actually on stage when actors pop the cork of a bottle of Moët et Chandon it will only contain a bland golden fizz, so that the performers don't get carried away and forget their lines.... but a sense of celebration surrounds the opening of a bottle of Champagne wherever and whenever it happens.

Of course it is expensive: that is part of the treat. Champagne signals the end of a First Night in the theatre, where bottles cool in dingy basins amongst bouquets in dark dressing rooms. It raises a humble cheese on toast supper into a feast, it greets us in the evening as we enter grand houses for dinner, and at midday in supermarkets at ribbon-cutting ceremonies. It is given in lovely oblong boxes, so easy to wrap, and carried carefully in a frosty sleeve to make a picnic unforgettable. From the pages that follow it is strangely touching to read how we all adore 'champers', and what a comfort is can be, and what joy it brings and what triumphs it proclaims.

After a massively long and arduous trek to find the longest source of the Nile, the crew and I, bitten and scratched and stung and exhausted, raised glasses of Champagne in the middle of the high forests of Rwanda: the company medic had slogged along for eight hours with a bottle in his rucksack, as nothing else would suffice to mark such an important achievement.

So here I am, sitting at my desk, and although it is still broad daylight I sense that the sun might already be over the yard arm, and it is time to feel the frisson of the chilled bottle in the hand, the thwonking pop of the cork, the soft swish of the pale gold liquid, the snap of the bubbles at the first sip, the sudden promise that all's right with the world, and if it isn't, what's wrong can always be fixed.

All hail, Champagne !! and cheers, sweeties !!

JOHN BURNINGHAM'S
CHAMPAGNE

"Champagne is co-extensive with civilisation, and, in the upper and middle classes of society, almost synonymous, except in France, with conviviality. It is a vehicle for French gaiety, and is prized because it carries with it something of the spirit of the people among whom it has its origin. At the dinner table, when too many guests seem almost apprehensive of being spoken to by some neighbour whose very name they have failed to catch, champagne breaks down the awkward reserve and banishes the oppressive silence. Timid eyelids are lifted, the unveiled eyes begin to sparkle, the monosyllables expand into sentences, and a welcome infusion of sans géne *lightens the stolidity of excellent but embarrassed guests. Something of the French spirit enters into the company, and everybody finds at least his gayer if not his better self. Thus we find that in the improvement of manners, as indicated by a smaller consumption of alcoholic liquors, which delights the temperance reformer, champagne still holds it own. Other wines may be dispensed with but champagne is indispensible,*

and the reason is that it brings the sunshine of France into a gloomy climate, and the light-heartedness of France into companies that are perhaps given to taking life too seriously. It is only France that knows the secret of these precious invisible exports, and humanity is her debtor for a perpetually renewed exhilaration."

The Times, 21st March 1911

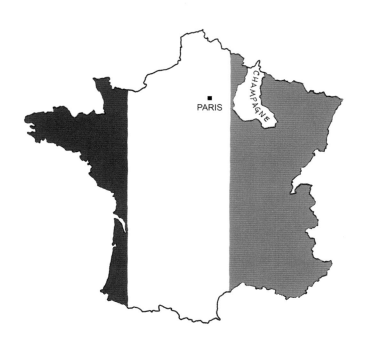

CHAMPAGNE comes from the Champagne region as you might expect. Any other white wine that produces bubbles, however delicious it may be, is known only as sparkling wine. It is not Champagne and must not be called Champagne.

The Champagne region is restricted to the three departments of Marne, Aisne and Aube within which the rights of wine growers are fiercely protected. Controls govern the varieties of grape used in Champagne: where they can be grown, the ranking of the vineyards, how and when the grapes are harvested, the method of manufacture, the labelling, the price.

Up to three grape varieties are used. Most dominant are the Pinot Noir and Pinot Meunier, which have red skins and white juice, but the white-skinned Chardonnay is also grown. The method underlying the art of Champagne making or blending – the cuvée – is a closely guarded secret of the individual Champagne houses and wine makers. It could take a blend of many wines from various vineyards, the addition of some sugar syrup, and several years to produce a Champagne.

The bottled drink has always been expensive. For Henri Krug, one-time doyen of the House of Krug, the cost was soon forgotten: 'You remember the taste for days, months, years and possibly for life' he said. 'But you forget how much you paid after a few minutes. I compare that to the kind of emotion you have when you go to the opera. I remember every minute of Don Giovanni conducted by Riccardo Muti and I forget how much I paid for my seat.' Champagne is associated with fun, luxury, and celebration:

births, engagements, weddings, New Year, the launch of a ship, songs, sporting victories. The pop of the cork and the spumante add to the intoxication. It has been calculated that around 11 million bubbles rise from one flute of Champagne – more bubbles than there are people living in New York.

Bornes (boundary markers)

How did Champagne get its fizz and popularity? There were vineyards in the chalky fields of Champagne when the Romans invaded. The name Champagne comes from Campania, the Latin for country. The Romans excavated the chalk from the soil, leaving pits (les crayeres) and tunnels that are now used to store, cool, and age the Champagne. Many miles of these tunnels lie beneath the headquarters of the big Champagne houses in Reims and Epernay. In wartime they were ideal for hiding the Champagne from the enemy.

In contrast to the sunny warmth of the grape-growing regions of Burgundy, the chalk soil and cool climate of the Champagne region created their own special conditions for making wine. The area became noted for its still wines. The closeness to Paris, the royal connection with the ancient city of Reims where eight French kings had been crowned in its cathedral, the vast parcels of land owned by nobility and merchants, each contributed to the success of the still wine from the Champagne region.

But in reality wine produced in Champagne has always had a natural tendency to bubble. This arises from a fermentation which is halted by the freezing winters and ice-cold cellars, and which resumes once it has warmed up a bit in the spring. The yeast and the sugars, naturally present in the wine, turn to alcohol during the second fermentation. This produces carbon dioxide which, when exposed to air and released, escapes as bubbles.

The story goes that when Dom Pérignon first put the bubbles in Champagne, having been appointed cellar master to the Abbey of Hautvillers in 1668, he declared, 'I have tasted the stars'. This delightful tale first emerged much later, just prior to the 1889 World Exhibition in Paris. Since then the image of the blind Benedictine abbot with his stick has always been associated with Moët and Chandon, and Dom Pérignon remains its bestselling brand of Champagne. It is closer to the truth to suggest that Dom Pérignon invented the art of blending wines. He certainly knew about the bubbles; all the wine makers in Champagne did. But he did his best to remove them because they were widely regarded as undesirable in late 17th century France.

Dom Pérignon produced wonderful wines that brought great wealth to his monastery. The wine for local use was bottled in thin, hand-blown French glass fired in wood ovens. Because these bottles did not easily withstand the pressure caused by the build-up of carbon dioxide, they often exploded. The waste and cost were damaging. It made better economic sense for the wine to be transported in wooden casks to England in particular. Once sealed in English bottles it could be exported safely to anywhere else. British glass, fired in coal-burning ovens, was both stronger and cheaper.

The merchants found that adding sugar and a little fortified brandy to the bottle improved the taste of the wine which had often soured and clouded. The wine was not the clear pale yellow colour of today but more a browny pink. When the bottle was opened there was a pleasing pop and an audible fizz. This was popular among its English society drinkers and the demand for vin mousseux, or sparkling wine, grew. French wine makers frowned on the English taste, but nevertheless took note and took orders.

The English played other parts in the story of Champagne. In 1662, before Dom Pérignon had been appointed cellar master at Hautvillers, the scientist Charles Merrett gave a lecture to the Royal Society in London. He explained how putting sugar in wine produced bubbles. The first mention of sparkling Champagne and its happy effect appear in a drinking song in *The Man of Mode*, a play that opened in London in 1676. Sir Fopling and his friends fill their glasses and sing:

> *To the Mall and the Park,*
> *Where we love till 'tis dark;*
> *Then sparkling Champagne*
> *Puts an end to their reign;*
> *It quickly recovers*
> *Poor languishing lovers;*
> *Makes us frolic and gay, and drowns all sorrow.*
> *But alas! we relapse again on the morrow.*

Whenever and wherever bubbling Champagne was discovered its appeal soon grew. England, Russia, Prussia, America, even the palace at Versailles wanted more. Because the Champagne region included the paths of two important trade routes, one running east to west the other north to south, it was well placed to meet the demand. These trade routes brought the region enormous wealth but they also brought war and occupation.

The Champagne region has been invaded by the Gauls, the Romans, Russians, Prussians, and twice by the Germans. With war came the blockades on the ports, various prohibitions and interruptions to the highly profitable trade in Champagne. Getting round these difficulties took daring and imagination. To avoid the blockade on ports in 1811 the merchant Charles-Henri Heidsieck rode on a white horse all the way from France to Russia, ahead of Napoleon's advancing army, to sell Champagne to the Imperial Court. He was rewarded for his brave effort with many sales and orders. His son, Charles Camille Heidsieck, better known as Champagne Charlie, would go on to found the Charles Heidsieck Company and to open up the American market.

> *Champagne Charlie is my name,*
> *Champagne drinking is my game.*

It was the Americans who gave Charles Heidsieck his nickname, the newspapers making much of him and his adventures. Times were good for Champagne Charlie until he was caught up in the American Civil War trying to recover some payments that were due. He was arrested in possession of documents from textile manufacturers intended for the Confederates and imprisoned as a spy. Many, including Napoleon III, appealed to Abraham Lincoln for his release. Although he was freed eventually he was ruined financially.

The Russians liked their Champagne sweet so an inexcusable amount of sugar was added. They were particularly fond of the specially sweetened Veuve Cliquot produced by the widow Madame Barbe-Nicole Cliquot. In 1806 it was unheard of for a woman to be a wine producer or indeed to run any large business. Later, other famous Champagne-producing widows gained acceptance: Louise Pommery later in the 19th century, Marie Louise Lanson de Nonancourt and Lily Bollinger in the 20th. But Madame Cliquot was the first and her signature Veuve Cliquot (Widow Cliquot) still appears on the yellow label non-vintage Champagne bearing her name.

As a child she had survived the long years of the French Revolution. Her family called Ponsardin who were wealthy textile merchants from Reims adapted to the times and sided with the revolutionaries. Their titled customers were now addressed as citoyens. Their daughter, Citoyen Barbe-Nicole Ponsardin, made a good marriage to the wealthy Citoyen Francois Cliquot. When the years of upheaval and terror ended in 1799 the appellation citoyen was dropped. Together the married couple started a wine business learning the difficult trade and selling the wine locally. This in itself was most unusual for a woman. It meant that when her husband Francois died of typhoid, or perhaps it was suicide, in 1805 Madame Barbe-Nicole Cliquot was well prepared to take on the business and a partner, which she did under the name of Veuve Cliquot Ponsardin & Co. And she was only 27. She is credited with experimenting with 'riddling' (turning the bottles by degrees) and with 'disgorgement' (the removal of sediment from the bottle). This was effected by storing the bottles at an angle tilted downwards so that the sediment sank into the neck of the bottle. When the bottle was opened the yeast sediment drained away. The space left behind was filled with a sugar syrup – the 'dosage' – and a top-up of another wine. These experiments greatly improved the clarity and taste. The year 1811 was brilliant for Madame Veuve Cliquot. A vintage Champagne is produced from grapes harvested in a single year. November 1811 was a perfect harvest - *vendange*, overlooked by the passage of a bright comet in the sky, which some saw as a favourable omen. After the pressing – gentle enough merely to release the white juice from the red-skinned grapes - the wine was left to age in her cellars. A minimum of three years for a vintage Champagne. It was known as the comet vintage - *vin de la comète*. At that time, there were no labels on bottles to identify the Champagne producer or the vintage but, in 1811, Madame Cliquot branded stars on the bottom of the corks of the comet vintage.

When the Russians invaded France in the winter of 1814, Madame Veuve Cliquot concealed the comet vintage in her cellars. She let the Russian officers drink other Champagne knowing time was on her side. 'Today they drink', she said. 'Tomorrow they will pay.' After a short while the French re-captured Reims and then it was the turn of Napoleon's troops to celebrate with Champagne. The story goes that Madame Veuve Cliquot handed glasses and bottles of Champagne to the officers on horseback. Unable to draw the corks, the officers lopped off the necks of the bottles with their sabres allowing the frothing Champagne to clear away any broken glass - an art called sabrage that is sometimes practised today. When Napoleon abdicated in 1815 Madame Veuve Cliquot saw an opportunity to open up trade in Russia before her competitors could exploit the lucrative market.

She chartered a private ship and loaded it with 10,550 bottles of Champagne including the comet vintage. When it sailed for the Baltic Sea, with her agent Louis Boehne on board, the blockade on the ports had just been lifted. The Russians loved the 1811 vintage with the comet cork. The entire stock was sold at huge prices and new orders

were placed. Another shipment of 12,780 bottles of the 1811 vintage was soon on its way. Just as Madame Cliquot had predicted, the Russians were now paying well for her Champagne. In Russia she was called Klikoskaya. The comet vintage had made her rich and famous.

> *Cliquot! Cliquot! That's the stuff to make you jolly*
> *Cliquot! Cliquot! Soon will banish melancholy.*
> *Cliquot! Cliquot! Drinking other wine is folly*
> *Cliquot! Cliquot! That's the drink for me.*

One of Madame Cliquot's comet vintage star-branded corks.

With the abdication of Napoleon Bonaparte, the Russians returned to Reims and, of course, celebrated with Champagne. So it was said that in Champagne the Napoleonic Wars ended with the popping of corks.

New routes opened up with the arrival of the railways. Champagne bottles no longer had to be taken by barge and wagons to the ports for shipment. In 1836 the consumption in France was 626,000 bottles. Abroad, consumption was (on average): 467,000 bottles in England and the East Indies; 479,000 in Germany; 400,000 in the United States; 288,000 in Russia; 30,000 in Sweden and Denmark combined. It was now easier for agents to reach new markets and for visitors to come to the Champagne region. Epernay was a stop on the Orient Express route to Paris where travellers could enjoy a glass of Champagne at the Buffet de la Gare.

Easier access to St Petersburg meant Veuve Cliquot had many competitors in Russia. Louis Roederer wooed Tsar Alexander II, Emperor of Russia, King of Poland and Grand Prince of Finland. (This was the Tsar who sold Alaska to the United States.) Mark Twain visited the Tsar on his travels and found him most affable with a noble face especially without his cap on. Tsar Alexander II wanted a Champagne blended just for him and put in a distinctive bottle so that he could see its contents and others could appreciate its exclusivity. So in 1876 Louis Roederer created Cristal Champagne - a special cuvée for the Tsar in a clear lead glass bottle with a flat bottom. Champagne is best kept in dark bottles because light can ruin it, and Champagne thus affected is called 'light struck'. Although Cristal Champagne has kept its distinctive shape and glass it comes wrapped in a special light-resistant cellophane.

Roederer's connection with the Tsars was not halted by the assassination of Alexander II in 1881. He continued to supply the next two Tsars until the Russian Revolution ended sales abruptly. When he came to power Stalin ordered the mass planting of vineyards as part of his Five-Year Plans but the sweet sparkling wine produced was unsuccessful. Roederer Cristal was not exported to Russia again until 1945. From that year sales continued smoothly until a Russian company selling a vodka called Kristal with a K took the French company to court over a dispute about the name, demanding that the Roederer company pay compensation. The argument was eventually resolved, and Cristal Champagne is now back in Russia to be enjoyed by thirsty oligarchs.

Hip hop artists and rappers also have a taste for Cristal Champagne. Perhaps it is the name. They call it Crissy. Cristal goes with bling, conspicuous consumption and alcoholic ejaculation. Later Jay-Z excluded Cristal from his clubs and videos. Instead he featured a non-vintage Champagne produced by the long-established but little known Cattier company: Armand de Brignac's Brut Gold 'Ace of Spades'. Since then sales of this Champagne have rocketed. In May 2013 a Jeroboam of Cristal Champagne dipped in gold was launched at Monaco's Billionaire Club for the Grand Prix. In the UK 200 Jeroboams of the gold-dipped Cristal Champagne were sold at a price of £18,000 each. Fortunes have been made by the big Champagne-producing houses, the grands marques, regardless of the ups and downs of the harvests. However, 'il n'est pas de roses sans épines' (there is no rose without thorns). In the early 20th century some Champagne houses began to import cheaper grapes from the south of France to increase profits so the local vignerons, the wine growers, struck. The strikers attacked the cellars and business premises, the houses and some of the vineyards as well. Bottles and casks were destroyed. In the

Ay district alone up to six million bottles of Champagne were smashed.

The strike in 1911 was not only about the use of cheap grapes from the south. It was a fight between the different départements of the area for commercial advantage. The Marne demanded exclusive claim to the name Champagne. This was challenged by the Aube and one or two other départements. The riot was taken up not just by the peasants and small growers, who were near starvation following two poor years, but by the local magistrates. It ended with the producers promising to use only the grapes from their region but the outbreak of the First World War brought about an abrupt change of focus.

On 18th September 1914 German shells hit the cathedral in Reims causing terrible damage and casualties. The summer of 1914 had promised an excellent vintage but in September, before the grapes could be harvested, the first Battle of the Marne began. Most of the fighting took place in the vineyards with the vines now laden with ripening fruit. For the next four years the front line lay

along the Vesle valley with the Champagne-making villages on the northern slopes of the Mountain of Reims in the firing line. It was left to the old men, women and children to tend the vines as best they could. More than

20 children were killed harvesting the grapes in two vine-yards belonging to Pommery & Greno during that autumn of 1914.

Alan Seeger, an American poet and soldier who fought in the First World War, wrote a poem – *Champagne, 1914-15* - which honoured those who fought and died there. It began:

> *In the glad revels, in the happy fetes,*
> *When cheeks are flushed, and glasses gilt and pearled*
> *With the sweet wine of France that concentrates*
> *The sunshine and the beauty of the world,*
> *Drink sometimes, you whose footsteps yet may tread*
> *The undisturbed, delightful paths of Earth,*
> *To those whose blood, in pious duty shed,*
> *Hallows the soil where that same wine had birth.*
> *Here, by devoted comrades laid away,*
> *Along our lines they slumber where they fell,*
> *Beside the crater at the Ferme d'Alger*
> *And up the bloody slopes of La Pompelle,*
> *And round the city whose cathedral towers*
> *The enemies of Beauty dared profane,*
> *And in the mat of multicoloured flowers*
> *That clothe the sunny chalk-fields of Champagne.*
> *Under the little crosses where they rise*
> *The soldier rests.*

Seeger died at the Battle of the Somme in July 1916. His Champagne poem ended:

> *Be mindful of the men they were, and raise*
> *Your glasses to them in one silent toast.*
> *Drink to them - amorous of dear Earth as well,*
> *They asked no tribute lovelier than this -*
> *And in the wine that ripened where they fell,*
> *Oh, frame your lips as though it were a kiss.*

War cemeteries for the soldiers – allies and enemies – of both world wars are a feature of today's gentle Champagne landscape.

Of course Champagne was smuggled abroad despite the blockades. The Swedish schooner, *the Jönköping,* was stopped in 1916 in the Baltic Sea by a German U-boat. Its chief cargo was some 2,000 bottles of Champagne, mostly 1907 vintage Heidsieck Goût Americain, destined for the Russian Imperial court. The Germans sank the wooden schooner and the wreck and its cargo lay undiscovered until 1997.

Champagne was looted too. The writer Arthur Ransome covering the war in Russia for the Daily News made his way to Rumania when it entered the war on the side of the Allies in 1916. After early Rumanian success, the German bombs and attacks forced a general retreat. Ransome got a lift out of Rumania with Colonel Thomson, who was the British Military Attaché in Bucharest. Climbing into the car Ransome found his knees under his chin.

> *'Have a look,' said Thomson, and I lifted the carpet to see that the floor of the car was covered with bottles of Champagne. Thomson, laughed. 'Well', he said, 'If it has got to be a retreat, I don't see why it should be a dry one.'*

The Autobiography of Arthur Ransome

After the First World War the ruination of the vineyards provided an opportunity for replanting with an American rootstock resistant to the devastating phylloxera disease. Sales of Champagne fell all the same - the Russian market was closed after the Revolution and the American market was closed by the 1920 prohibition order. Even so some bottles got through. For example a couple of Americans searching for clams along the shore spotted nine bottles in the water. They turned out to be bootlegged Heidsieck Extra Dry 1920.

The Germans had always been big importers of Champagne. With the outbreak of the Second World War a Führer of Champagne, Herr Klaebisch, was appointed and given an office in Reims to oversee the production. He set up a regulatory body called the Comité Interprofessionnel du Vin de Champagne (CIVC) with the Frenchman Comte Robert-Jean de Vogue as its chief.

Although sales of Champagne to civilians without permission were forbidden Champagne production was allowed to continue with a permit. Up to 400,000 bottles were dispatched each week to German armed forces on all fronts with priority given to the Luftwaffe and the Navy. The Champagne was not the best - indeed it was often made almost undrinkable. Bottles bound for Germany were doctored as well. Once again the cellars and tunnels beneath Epernay and Reims were used to hide the best Champagne alongside soldiers and the French Resistance.

In 1943 Comte de Vogue was arrested by the Gestapo and condemned to death by a German military court in Reims. Deported to Germany he worked in the labour camps until they were liberated by the British in 1945. Joseph Krug II of Krug Champagne and his wife were also arrested by the Gestapo but were released. Madame Jeanne Krug was later re-arrested and imprisoned.

Victory was of course celebrated with Champagne. In Reims the German commander, Alfred Jodl, offered an unconditional surrender to General Dwight D Eisenhower on May 7 1945. The next morning the signing was celebrated with six cases of the 1934 vintage of Pommery.

After the war the CIVC chief, Comte Robert-Jean de Vogue, was made Commander of the Legion of Honour, and given the Croix de Guerre and other medals for his part in the resistance in which he had rallied both the vigneron and the big Champagne houses to resist the German occupation. Later de Vogue joined Moët and Chandon and became its Managing Director. Jeanne Krug was awarded the Medaille de la Resistance.

Champagne is still a drink of war. When the United States boycotted French wines after France refused to join the action against Iraq Champagne was the exception. Indeed, sales of Champagne to the US increased. Reims and Epernay and the Champagne villages recovered from the war years. Eighteen firms, or Grandes Marques, now supply around 65 per cent of all Champagne production. Markets change. Britain is set to be the biggest importer of Champagne overtaking Germany and America. The Chinese have developed a taste for Champagne. As well as importing vast quantities they are creating vineyards for the making of sparkling wine. They have agreed not to call it Champagne. Nigerians also like their Champagne. Their 2011 Champagne consumption reached 8bn naira (£31m) and was the fastest growing rate of new consumption in the

CHAMPAGNE IN THE GRAPE: PROMISE OF A RARE VINTAGE YEAR.

world, ahead of Brazil, China and the established markets such as America and Australia.

Tastes change as well. Napoleon III hated the sweet Veuve Cliquot preferring the drier Champagne enjoyed by the English and produced by another French widow, Louise Pommery. Winston Churchill liked Pol Roger. President Mobuto is said to have been partial to Dom Pérignon. The author Jeffrey Archer drinks only Krug at his summer parties. The artist Ronald Searle chose Cristal Champagne for his luxury on Desert Island Discs. He added that he would put a note asking for another in a bottle and throw it into the sea.

American Taste or 'Goût Americain' was created in the early 1900s by Heidseck & Co Monopole for the American market which preferred a dry Champagne. English Taste or 'Goût Anglais' refers to an extra-dry Champagne to the horror of some French producers. Whatever your 'goût', here are some Champagne moments.

"Come quickly, I am tasting the stars!"

Dom Pérignon

Believed to have been said by Dom Pérignon, Benedictine monk (1638-1715) and cellar master at the Abbey of Hautvillers, on inventing Champagne. Dom Pérignon did not invent Champagne but he was a highly skilled wine maker. It was just an appealing story that has helped to boost sales. Today Dom Pérignon is Moët & Chandon's bestselling vintage Champagne.

*"In victory you deserve Champagne,
in defeat you need it."*

Napoleon Bonaparte

PHEASANT SHOOTING

Close by the borders of the fringed lake,
And on the oak's expanding bough is seen,
What time the leaves the passing zephyrs shake,
And sweetly murmur thro' the sylvan scene.

The gaudy pheasant, rich with varying dyes,
That fade alternate, and alternate glow;
Receiving now her colour from the skies,
And now reflecting back the wat'ry bow.

He flaps his wings, erects his spotted crest,
His flaming eyes dart forth a piercing ray;
He swells the lovely plumage of his breast,
And glares a wonder on the orient day.

Ah! what avails such heavenly plumes as thine,
When dogs and sportsmen in thy ruin join.

The Casket, Philadelphia, 1828

*"The Regiment of Champagne bottles
are terribly mutinous and excitable."*

Charles Dickens, 1855

The hand blown French glass fired in wood ovens did not easily withstand the pressure caused by the build up of carbon dioxide gas and frequently exploded.

TSAR ALEXANDER II

Louis Roederer, the producer of the famous brand of Crystal, was supplying the Tsar Alexander II of Russia with Champagne. At that time the political situation was very unstable in Russia and the Tsar feared he would get killed. In 1876 he ordered Roederer to send Champagne using transparent bottles so no one could hide a bomb in one of the bottles. Since then Roederer has only used only clear lead crystal Champagne bottles with flat bottoms.

L. & L. Hunt Club dinner –

Stag and Garter Hotel,
LINLITHGOW.

| Job and Post Horses. |  | Waggonettes, Gigs. &c. |

T. M. WOODCOCK.

1878

					£	s	d
Novr	1	10 dinners @ 10/–			5		
		Corkage					
	4	Bottles Champagne	@ 2/6			10	
	13	other Bottles	@ 1/6			19	6
		Dessert			1	10	
		Tea & Coffee				7	6
		Attendance			1		
				£	9	7	0

J. M. Woodcock

10/11/79
£9–7–0

38

DINNER FOR TEN AT THE STAR AND GARTER HOTEL
(including four bottles of Champagne and 13 other bottles)

CHAMPAGNE CHARLIE

I've seen a deal of gaiety throughout my noisy life,
With all my grand accomplishments I ne'er could get a wife;
The thing I most excel in is the PRFG game,
A noise all night, in bed all day, and swimming in Champagne.

[Chorus]
For Champagne Charlie is my name,
Champagne Charlie is my name;
Good for any game at night, my boys,
Good for any game at night my, boys,
Champagne Charlie is my name,
Champagne Charlie is my name;
Good for any game at night boys,
Who'll come and join me in a spree?

The way I gained my title's by a hobby which I got
Of never letting others pay, however long the shot;
Whoever drinks at my expense are treated all the same,
From dukes, lords, to cabmen down, I make them drink Champagne.
[Chorus]

From coffee and from supper rooms, from Poplar to Pall Mall,
The girls on seeing me, exclaim, "O, what a Champagne swell!"
The notion 'tis of every one, if 'twere not for my name,
And causing so much to be drunk, they'd never make Champagne.
[Chorus]

Some epicures like burgundy, hock, claret and moselle,
But Moet's vintage only satisfies this Champagne swell,
What matters if to bed I go and head is mud all thick,
A bottle in the morning sets me right then very quick.
[Chorus]

Perhaps you fancy what I say is nothing else but chaff,
And only done, like other songs, to merely raise a laugh;
To prove that I am not in jest, each man a bottle of Cham.
I'll stand fiz round, yes that I will, and stand it like a lamb.
[Chorus]

40

RIGHT: *George Leybourne,*
the music hall artist, was
best known for this Victo-
rian song "Champagne
Charlie" which he wrote and
performed dressed as a swell
in top hat and tails. The
original Champagne Charlie
was the wine merchant
Charles Heidsieck.

OVERLEAF: *The Black*
Crooke Co, 1893. All
female theatre company.

TO THE NORTH POLE

In 1896 Fridtjof Nansen returned to Norway a hero
after leading an expedition towards the North Pole.
They had journeyed by ship and dog sledge and reached
100 miles short of the North Pole. This achievement
was the closest any explorer had been to the Pole and it
had taken them two years.

The Swedish aeronaut, Salomon Andrée, thought the
journey could be done in six days in a hydrogen balloon.
The balloon would be launched from land and carried
north by air currents across the polar sea and ice over the
North Pole and back south. That was the plan but in case
they were obliged to land they would stow sledges and a
boat in the car of the balloon for their return.

Funds were raised for the journey and for the specially
adapted balloon. It was housed on Dane's Island. On 11th
July 1897 the three aeronauts, Salomon Andrée, photographer Nils Strindberg and Knut Fraenkel, breakfasted on
board the Svenskund with the ship's chief and the doctor.
The chief brought in a bottle of Champagne and a toast
was raised to their journey. After a few last checks the
aeronauts climbed into the car of the balloon and the ropes
were cut. The Eagle rose to great cheers from the onlookers
but then alarmingly began to sink, touched the sea,
bounced up again and disappeared from view.

Next day Andrée wrote in his diary: "It is not a little
strange to be floating here above the Polar Sea. To be the
first that have floated here in a balloon. How soon I wonder shall we have successors? Shall we be thought mad or
will our example be followed? I cannot deny but that all
three of us are dominated by a feeling of pride. We think
we can well face death, having done what we have done…"

Cloud and fog closed in cooling the balloon, icing the rig-
ging and guide ropes, dragging down its height and speed.

They may have been losing gas too. The weather worsened and the balloon began to bump along the ice until on the morning of 14th July the decision was taken to land. The flight had lasted 65 hours, covered 517 miles, and was over 400 miles short of the North Pole.

There was nothing for it but to prepare for the march back across the sea ice, packing and repacking the sledges, reducing their load as much as possible. A bottle of Champagne, brought for a celebration, was opened. They drank it with biscuits and honey, as Andrée's diary records:

27th July: 'On bivouacking eat in the tent. Champagne, biscuits and honey. I swept the tent with the strawcap of the Champagne bottle.'

Next morning the Swedish flag was raised above the sledges along with a shout of hurrah and they set off across the floating sea ice.

It wasn't until 1930 that a party from a Norwegian ship came ashore on White Island and found the remains of Andrée and Fraenkel and the carefully preserved records of their journey. Strindberg's body was found later in a grave.

Extracts from *The Andrée Diaries*, trs by Edward Adams-Ray. John Lane, Bodley Head 1931.

OVERLEAF: *A hard landing. The end of the Swedish expedition to the North Pole by balloon.*

OSCAR WILDE

Mr Edward Carson, QC:

Do you drink Champagne yourself?

Mr Oscar Wilde:

Yes, iced Champagne is a favourite drink of mine – strongly against my doctor's orders.

Mr Edward Carson, QC:

Never mind your doctor's orders, sir!

Mr Oscar Wilde:

I never do.

From the 1895 trials of Oscar Wilde

SIR WINSTON CHURCHILL

Dean Acheson recalled Clementine telling him that
Churchill "always had his own bottle of Champagne by
his place at the table, to be independent of the vagaries of
butlers". It is reasonable to assume that the bottle was of
the since-discontinued 50 cl size, which Churchill preferred
to the 75 cl bottle now commonly sold. "A single glass of
Champagne," Churchill wrote in 1898, "imparts a feeling
of exhilaration. The nerves are braced, the imagination is
agreeably stirred, the wits become more nimble". He
quickly added, "A bottle produces the opposite effect."

Frederick Lindemann was Professor of Physics at Oxford and a friend of Churchill, who made him his chief scientific adviser during the war and a peer, Lord Cherwell. Churchill liked him because he was able to explain complex scientific problems in simple terms. "Whipping out his slide-rule the Prof [as Churchill always called him] would make lightning calculations about anything from economic statistics to the volume of water Churchill would need to make an impressive cascade. Lindemann once [during the 1930s] worked out how much Champagne his friend had drunk in his life-time – Churchill was disappointed to learn that it was only enough in bottles to fill half a railway carriage."

At the Paris World Fair in 1900 the Champagne house
Mercier tethered a balloon which could carry ten people and
rise to 300 metres. This was a brilliant piece of early advertising by Mercier. Visitors to the Fair could see the balloon in
the air above the crowds with the Mercier name emblazoned
on it in three metre high letters. Those brave enough to
ascend in the balloon paid five francs for the ride and were
given Champagne to drink. The plan was that at the end of
the Fair in November the balloon would be released and the
aeronaut would pilot it back to Epernay in Champagne.

For a time they could see Epernay but then winds carried them back north and they were obliged to land in a field in Belgium. The local policeman found six bottles of Champagne and promptly charged the pilot with importing Champagne without a licence. Eugène Mercier later said:

C'est la publicité la moins chère que j'ai jamais faite. La relation de cette aventure dans la presse me revient à moins. (It's the cheapest advertising I've ever done. Telling the story in the newspaper cost me nothing.)

DIRTY BERTIE

Le Chabanais, founded in 1878 by Irish-born Madame Kelly, was considered the best and most luxurious brothel in Paris and was lavishly decorated in Moorish, Japanese and Louis XVI. It was reported to have cost 1.7 million francs. Though overtaken by One Two Two in the mid 1920s it nonetheless continued to run successfully for a further 25 years until its closure in 1946 when brothels were outlawed in France.

Regular visitors to Le Chabanais included Toulouse-Lautrec who painted 16 tableaux for the house, Guy de Maupassant who fashioned a replica of its Moorish room in his house by the sea so that he wouldn't miss it during his vacations there, and various prominent actors and dignitaries including Cary Grant, Humphrey Bogart, Mae West, Marlene Dietrich, the Maharajah of Kapurthala and King Carlos I of Portugal.

BELOW: *The chair made especially for Bertie's pleasure for use at Le Chabanais.*

Most notably, "Bertie", Prince of Wales, who would later become King Edward VII of the United Kingdom, was an habituée (frequent patron) of the establishment and one of the rooms carried his coat of arms over the bed. In this room was a large copper bath-tub with a half-woman-half-swan figurehead that he had filled with Champagne which they afterwards consumed. In 1951 when the contents of La Chabanais were sold at auction the copper bath was bought by the antiques dealer Jacob Street, who later sold it to Salvador Dali in 1972 for 112,000 Francs (the equivalent of approximately £11,000 today). Dali had it placed in his room at the Hotel Meurice.

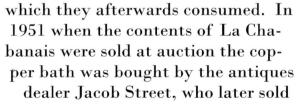

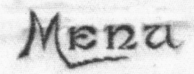

Menu

Dîner offert par le Président de la République Française
à S. M. ÉDOUARD VII
Le 2 Mai 1903

———

Crème Windsor

Oxtail Soup

Barquettes d'Ecrevisses Nantua

Truite Saumonée au Vin de Chambertin

Baron d'Agneau de Pauillac aux Morilles

Salmis de Gelinottes au Xérès

Canetons de Rouen à l'Archiduc

Sorbets au Kummel

Spooms au Cherry Brandy

Poulardes du Mans Truffées

Foie Gras frais à la Souvaroff

Salade Gauloise

Asperges d'Argenteuil sauce Mousseline

Petits Pois nouveaux à la Française

Timbales de Fruits Glacés à l'Orange

Glace Viviane

Feuilletés aux Amandes

Corbeilles de Fruits

———

Porto Commandador

Chablis Moutonne

Château Yquem 1874

Château Haut-Brion 1877

Mouton Rothschild 1875

Clos de Vougeot 1870

Moët Chandon White Seal

Moët et Chandon brut Impérial 1889

EDWARD VII

Dinner given by the President of the French Republic to His Majesty Edward VII.

CHAMPAGNE
ON ICE

Bastille Day, 14 July 1904
To celebrate Bastille Day, Ernest
Gourdon (left) enjoys a glass of
Mumm Champagne on ice with
the photographer Paul Pléneau
(right). The ship, *the Français,*
was blocked by ice by Booth
Island forcing the team to wait
out the winter.

Jean-Baptiste Charcot, Explorateur des
mers, navigateur des pôles © 2006
Editions Glénat. "Gourdon et Pléneau
autour d'une coupe de Champagne".

A HONEYMOON

June 1908

An idea for our honeymoon. Peter has offered me the use of his caravan. It's on the coast of Dorset. There are two tents in it and some Champagne and plenty of blankets. Shall we go there for a week and bathe?

From a letter from Kathleen Bruce to Captain Robert Scott.

25th December, Christmas Day, 1910

We had Champagne and drank Absent Dear Ones. I went to bed on the upper deck and told the stars how bursting and heavy my heart was.

From Kathleen Scott from aboard the *SS Morea* to Captain Scott, comander of the Antarctic polar expedition, 28th December, 1910.

Obs. 69 degrees 5' S., 178 degrees 30'E

My dearest girl. Christmas was more or less cheerful. Dinner with soup, stewed penguin, roast beef, plum pudding and mince pies, asparagus, Champagne and liqueurs. Afterwards, everyone sang. Very little talent.

From Captain Scott to his wife Kathleen from aboard the *Terra Nova* which was held up by ice in the Antarctic sea.

TO THE SOUTH POLE

MIDWINTER

CROUTE EREBUS   AMANDES SELLÉ
CREME DE VOLLAILE FERRAR

NOISETTES D'AGNEAU DARWINIAN

CENTRE FILLET DE BOEUF RÔTI
ASPERGES EN BRANCHES
POMMES DE TERRE NATURAL

POUDIN NOEL   PATÉ D'EUNICE
COMPOTE DE FRUITS

CHARLOTTE RUSSE GLACÉ À LA
BEARDMORE
BUZZARD'S CAKE
DESSERT.

CAPE EVANS.
1912.

Menu to celebrate Midwinter Day, 22nd June 1912.

LEFT: *At Cape Evans. Officers (left to right): A Cherry-Garrard, C S Wright, Dr E Atkinson, E W Nelson and T Gran. Nelson gave each a cardboard menu card shaped and painted like an Adélie penguin. Toasts were drunk in Champagne. After the dinner a decision was made to try to discover the fate of Capt Scott's polar party.*

Champagne Country

Map of Champagne Country
by Gilbert Rumbold from
The Savoy Cocktail Book,
published 1930.

Sacy

Venteul.

Damcry

Cumieres

Boursault

Clos l'Abbé

Vinay

Pierry

Cuis

CHAMPAGNE RIOTS

The extraordinary wine war in France was brought about in a somewhat curious manner. Not very long ago wine growers of the Marne petitioned the Government complaining that certain firms of the Aube were importing wines into the district that they might be mixed with genuine Champagne and sold as Champagne. Thereupon it was officially shown that there was likelihood of a law being passed that only wines grown in specified districts in the Marne should be sold as Champagne. There followed immediately such strenuous protests in the rival department, the Aube, that the Government showed signs of not making the law in question. Then, naturally, the Marne rose in its wrath. The sabotage of the rioters was only stopped by the drafting of a very great number of troops into the affected area, and there remains fear of further trouble.

The so-called "Wine Jacquerie" in the Champagne country reached an extraordinary pitch, and there must have been times when the French Government wondered when the "Jacques Bonhomme" of the affair was to appear and declare war to the death. Fortunately, at the moment, the troubles seem to be subsiding; though it is, of course, impossible to say whether fresh outbreaks will occur. The damage done has been very great. Probably, it will amount to well over a million pounds. The premises of such famous firms as Messrs. Deutz and Geldermann, Ayala, and Bissinger, to name a few of several, were burnt or otherwise wrecked. At Ay alone, at least six million bottles of Champagne have been smashed. The case of Mme. Bissinger is particularly hard, for that lady has at various times given some hundred thousands of francs to the town of Ay.

The Illustrated London News, 22nd April, 1911

THE WINE JACQUERIE: THE CHAMPAGNE RIOTS.

PHOTOGRAPHS BY BRANGER, TOPICAL, C. N., ILLUS. BUREAU, AND DELIUS.

FIRED BY MALCONTENTS: THE PREMISES OF MESSRS. DEUTZ AND GELDERMANN, AT AY, WELL ALIGHT.

SABOTAGE AT THE PRIVATE HOUSE OF A WINE-GROWER: MME. BISSINGER'S RESIDENCE ON FIRE.

AFTER A LOSS SET DOWN AT £300,000: THE BROTHERS AYALA LOOKING AT THEIR BURNT-OUT PREMISES.

A PART OF THE ENORMOUS DAMAGE DONE TO THE PREMISES OF MESSRS. AYALA: IN THE BURNT-OUT AREA.

THE SPILLING OF MUCH GOOD WINE: BOTTLES OF CHAMPAGNE SMASHED BY THE RIOTERS.

SOME OF THE SIX MILLION: BROKEN BOTTLES OF CHAMPAGNE IN THE GALLOIS CELLARS.

THOMAS WILLIAM BURGESS

For 36 years after Capt Webb first swam the Channel,
there were many attempts to equal his achievement, but
none succeeded until, in 1911, a 16-stone, bearded York-
shireman called Thomas Burgess made his 13th attempt. His
preparations were uncomplicated. The boat *Elsie* accompa-
nied him, the passengers included his official photographer.
Champagne, Swiss milk chocolate, cold chicken and grapes
were taken aboard for him to consume during his epic swim.
Save for a pair of motorist's goggles; he would swim naked,
despite the presence of ladies on shore and jellyfish once he
was under way. Smeared with lard, Burgess set out from
Dover shortly after 11am, quickly becoming seasick in the
choppy waters. However, the crew of a passing coaster
cheered him on and his boat sang and told jokes to keep his
spirits up.

With true Yorkshire grit, he persisted and just before 10am the following day, after almost 23 hours, he stepped onto French soil, still naked, to be greeted by a crowd of admiring Frenchmen. Burgess then drank some more of his Champagne.

Ian Mather, *Country Life,* 4th December, 2013

The *Titanic* was not launched with a bottle of Champagne cracked across her bow. And there was no dignitary to name the ship. Instead on 31st May 1911 in the Harland & Wolff shipyard in Belfast where the ship was built, the Chairman, Lord Pirrie, gave the order to the foreman for the launch of the world's biggest liner. Some see this as the Champagne curse but in fact none of the ships owned by the White Star Line (which owned the *Titanic)* was launched with Champagne or given a naming ceremony. The *Titanic* then spent almost a year being fitted out and undergoing sea trials.

For its maiden voyage from Southampton to New York there was plenty of Champagne on board for its first class passengers. Some 1,500 champagne glasses and 1,000 bottles of wine including Champagne were stored on board. The chief Champagne was Heidsieck & Co's Monopole Blue Top Champagne brut.

The ship set sail on 10th April 1912 and struck an iceberg in the North Atlantic at 11.40 pm on 14th April, and sank in the early hours next morning.

CHAROCHKA

That night I heard her sing for the first time, and the memory of those great deep notes, which are the secret of the best women gypsy singers will remain with me until I die. That night, too, I drank my first "charochka" to her singing. For a novice it is rather a trying ordeal. A large Champagne glass is filled to the brim. The gypsy singer places it on a plate and, facing the guest who is to drink the "charochka", sings the following verses:

> *"Like a scented flower*
> *Breathing out perfume,*
> *Bring the brimming glass;*
> *Let us drink a toast to Román,*
> *Román our beloved,*
> *And until he drinks it down*
> *Pour him out no more."*

The last four lines are a chorus, which is taken up with increasing frenzy by the whole troupe. The singer then advances towards the guest whom she is honouring, and holds out the plate to him. He takes the glass, bows low, stands erect, and then drinks the bumper in one draught, replacing the glass upside down on the plate to show that he has not left a drop.

It is an intimate ritual. Only the guest's Christian name is used, and, as there is no Robert in Russian, there and then Maria Nikolaievna christened me Román , which is the Russian equivalent, and Román or Rómocchka I have remained to my Russian friends ever since.

R.H. Bruce Lockhart, *Memoirs of a British Agent*

77

ANTON CHEKHOV

"The fact was we had saved up two bottles of Champagne, Champagne of the real sort with the label 'Veuve Clicquot' on the bottle. I had won this treasure that autumn in a bet at a christening party. It sometimes happens that during an arithmetic lesson, when the very atmosphere seems heavy with tedium, a butterfly will flutter into the classroom from out-of-doors, then the urchins will all crane their necks and follow its flight with curiosity, as if they saw before them something strange and new and not simply a butterfly. We were amused in just such a way by this ordinary Champagne which had dropped by chance into the midst of our dull life at the station. We said not a word and kept looking first at the clock and then at the bottles.

When the hands pointed to five minutes to twelve I slowly began to uncork one of the bottles. Whether I was weak from the effects of vodka or whether the bottle was moist I know not; I only remember that when the cork flew up to the ceiling with a pop the bottle slipped from my hands and fell to the floor. Not more than half a glassful of wine was spilled, for I was able to catch the bottle and to stop its fizzing mouth with my finger.

'Well, a happy New Year!' I cried, pouring out two glasses. 'Drink!'

My wife took the glass and stared at me with startled eyes. Her face had grown pale and was stamped with horror. 'Did you drop the bottle?' she asked.

'Yes; what of it?'

'That is bad,' she said, setting down her glass. 'It is a bad omen. It means some disaster will befall us this year.'

'What a peasant you are!' I sighed. 'You are an intelligent woman, but you rave like an old nurse. Drink!'

'God grant I may be raving, but – something will surely happen. You'll see.'

She did not finish her glass but went off to one side lost in thought. I made a few time-honoured remarks on the subject of super-stition, drank half the bottle, walked back and forth across the room, and went out."

Champagne, from *Stories of Russian Life*, by Anton Chekhov, trs. Marian Fell, pub Duckworth (1914)

In the summer of 1904, Anton Chekhov travelled to the spa town of Badenweiler in Germany where he was to be treated by Doctor Schwoerer for the advanced stages of tuberculosis. The night of 14th July was very hot and Chekhov's breathing became laboured. Dr Schwoerer was summoned and he ordered a bottle of Champagne from the hotel's reception. It was, a student called Rabeneck later wrote, a gesture from one doctor to another when all hope is lost.

'Ich sterbe', I am dying, said Chekhov. The cork was popped. Chekhov took the glass, drank the Champagne, turned on his side and shortly afterwards died. According to his wife, the Russian actress Olga Knipper, the silence was disturbed by a big black moth that flew in drawn by the electric lights, and fluttered wildly about.

September 1914 – First Battle of the Marne

After some early victories, the German army crossed the River
Marne in Champagne. Most of the fighting over the ten days of the
battle took place in the vineyards. It resulted in a great victory for
the Allies and stopped the Germans from reaching the Seine and
Paris. The October 1914 harvest produced an excellent vintage.
Great suffering and loss followed over the next four years when the
front line stuck in Champagne. Old men, women and children left to
tend the grapes lost their lives too, including 20 children working in
two Pommery & Greno vineyards in 1914, close to No-Man's Land.

RIGHT: *Christmas Post*

80

WEIHNACHTSPOST

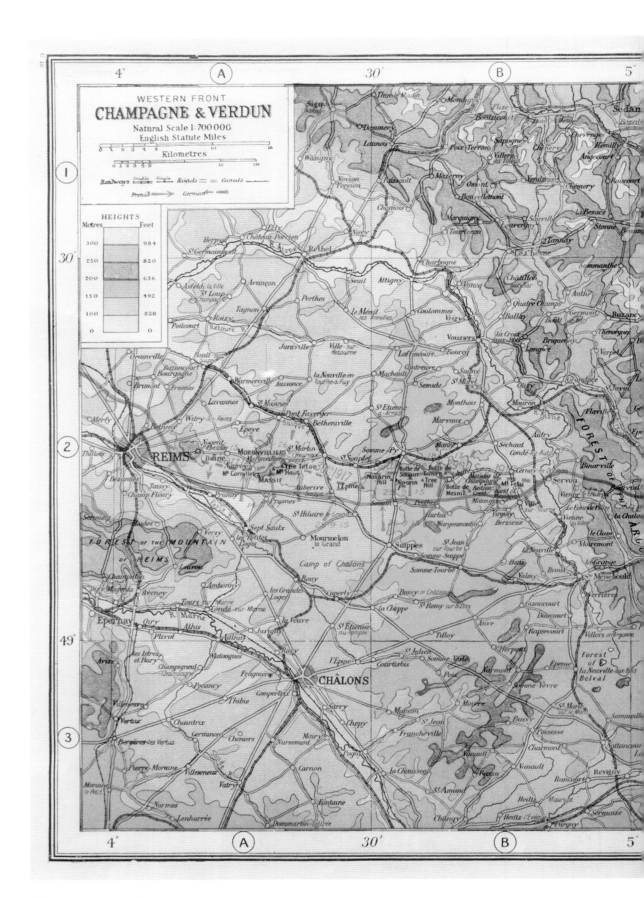

82   Champagne region map.

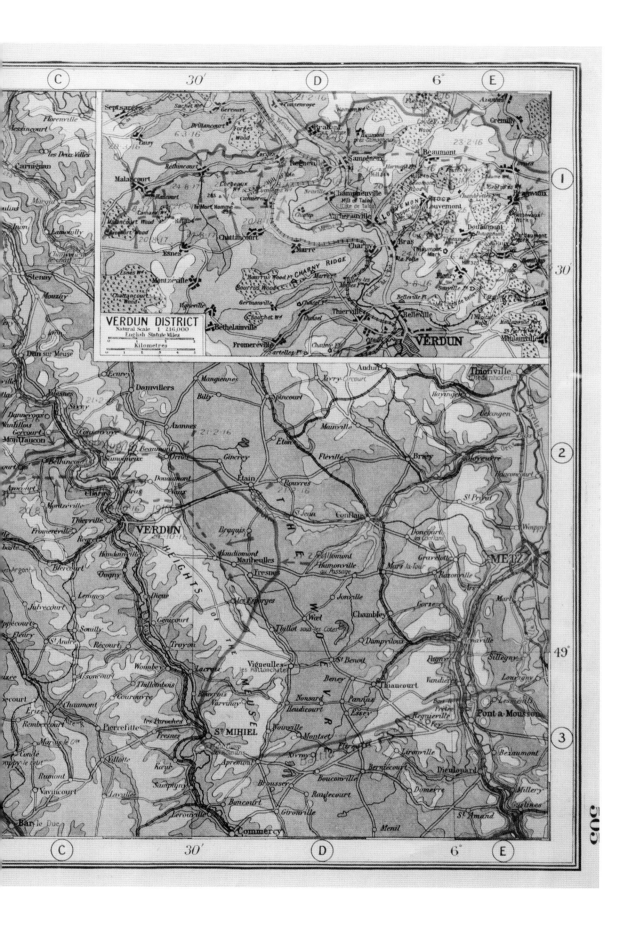

VERDUN DISTRICT
Natural Scale 1 : 216,000
English Statute Miles
Kilometres

ABOVE: *The graves of French soldiers killed in the Battle of the Marne in 1914.*

"Under the little crosses where they rise
The soldier rests. Now round him undismayed
The cannon thunders, and at night he lies
At peace beneath the eternal fusillade.

Be mindful of the men they were, and raise
Your glasses to them in one silent toast.
Drink to them — amorous of dear Earth as well,
They asked no tribute lovelier than this —
And in the wine that ripened where they fell,
Oh, frame your lips as though it were a kiss."

From *Champagne, 1914-1915* by Alan Seeger

Buck's Club is a gentlemen's club established in London in June 1919 and located at 18 Clifford Street, W1. P G Wodehouse mentions it in some stories and modelled his Drones Club mostly after Buck's. It is probably best known for the Buck's Fizz cocktail, created there in 1921 by its bartender, McGarry.

"Champagne and orange juice is a great drink. The orange improves the Champagne. The Champagne definitely improves the orange."

Allegedly overheard at a wedding,
HRH The Duke of Edinburgh

*"Before I was born my mother was in great
agony of spirit and in a tragic situation.
She could take no food except iced oysters
and Champagne. If people ask me when
I began to dance, I reply, in my mother's
womb, probably as a result of the oysters
and Champagne, the food of Aphrodite."*

Isadora Duncan, American choreographer
and dancer (1878-1927)

"If the aunt of the vicar has never touched liquor,
watch out when she finds the Champagne."

Rudyard Kipling (1865-1936)

ZELLI'S NIGHT CLUB

Paris 1929: The American dancer and film star, Louise Brooks, at Joe Zelli's nightclub, Royal Box, at 16 Rue Fontaine in Montmartre. At that time, Louise Brooks was the star of a German film, *Pandora's Box*, in which she played the central figure Lulu. Her bob haircut was much copied.

Behind them are drawings of clients by an Italian caricaturist called Zito. Below them was the dance floor. The Champagne was sold only by the bottle and the club's hostesses and gigolos were paid according to the numbers of bottles sold.

The cabaret club was very popular with the Americans who came to Paris in the Twenties. But the Wall Street crash in 1929, when this photograph was taken, and the depression soon had their effect on Zelli's business interests in France and America. The Royal Box closed in 1931.

AT JOE ZELLI'S WITH THE ROYAL BOX SMILE
PARIS, OCT. 28. 1929

COLETTE

"I was very well brought up. As convincing proof of such a categorical assertion, let me say that when I was barely three years of age my father, who believed in gentle and progressive methods, gave me a full liqueur glass of reddish-brown wine sent to him from his native Southern France, the Muscat wine of Frontignan.

It was like a sun-stroke, or love at first sight, or the sudden realisation of a nervous system; this consecration made me a worthy disciple of Wine forever afterwards. A little later I learned to quaff my glass of mulled wine, aromatic with cinnamon and lemon, to a dinner of boiled chestnuts. At the age when one can barely read I was spelling out drop by drop, red Burgundies, old and light, and dazzling Yquems. Champagne passed in its turn, a murmur of foam, leaping pearls of air, across birthday dinners and first communion festivities: with it came grey Puisaye truffles .... A fine lesson from which I acquired familiar and discreet knowledge of wine, not swallowed greedily, but measured out into narrow glasses, absorbed in mouthfuls with long spaces in between, and carefully reflected upon."

Colette, for Maison Nicolas, reprinted in *The Savoy Cocktail Book*, 1930.

BROOKLYN BRIDGE CELLAR

In the massive granite anchorage which held the suspension cables of the Brooklyn Bridge on the Manhattan side of New York's East River there used to be a Champagne cellar rented to Anthony Oechs & Co. It was built in 1876, seven years before the construction of the bridge was complete.

The temperature in the cellar was just right for the storage of vintage Champagne. Just visible on the back arch of the cellar is the Pol Roger sign. In a niche at the entrance to the cellar there was a statue of the Virgin Mary that had been brought over from the Pol Roger cellars in Epernay in Champagne. It was known as the Blue Grotto.

It was in 1919 that the temporary Wartime Prohibition Act banning alcohol of a certain strength came into effect in the United States on June 30th, with the following day, July 1st, becoming known as the "Thirsty First". This was followed by the banning of the manufacture and sale of all alcohol nationwide cross the United States, which lasted from 1920 until 1933 when it was repealed. For the whole of this prohibition period the Brooklyn cellar could not be used for the storage of Champagne.

Prohibition did not work. Instead it promoted a huge rise in organised crime and bootlegging, with illegal alcohol being sold through New York's speakeasy clubs.

When Prohibition was finally lifted in 1933 there was a great party in the cellar to celebrate the return of the keys to Anthony Oechs by Aldermanic President, Bernard S Deutsch.

"You step off the subway at Brooklyn bridge, turn sharp left through an underground passageway and pass through a cave-like door into medieval France," reported the *Pittsburgh Post-Gazette*. Still visible on the walls were popular sayings such as – "Who loveth not wine, women and song, he remaineth a fool his whole life long."

OPPOSITE: *Brooklyn Bridge, Wine Cellar 1992.* © *Stanley Greenberg/Esto.*

THE BROOKLYN ANCHORAGE.

96

The net paid circulation
for November exceeded
Daily – 1,450,000
Sunday– 2,000,000

DAILY ☒ NEWS

Copyright, 1933, by News Syndicate Co., Inc. Reg. U. S. Pat. Off. **NEW YORK'S** PICTURE NEWSPAPER

Entered as 2nd class matter
Post Office, New York, N. Y.

Vol. 15. No. 140   60 Pages   New York, Wednesday, December 6, 1933*

2 CENTS
IN CITY LIMITS

2 Cents | IN CITY LIMITS | 3 CENTS Elsewhere

YOU CAN DRINK!
REPEAL VOTED

—Story on Page **3**.

(NEWS photo)
Crowd pours into wine store of H. T. Dewey & Sons to purchase their first bottles of legal wine.

The Smile of Victory! Cameraman caught Al Smith, pioneer Repealist, in office at Empire State Building just as news was flashed of Utah's ratification. (NEWS photo)

Here's mud in your eye! Literary lights drink toast at Marlborough Club celebration. L. to r., seated: Mrs. Everadus Bogardus, Franklin P. Adams, Alison Smith, Alva Johnson, Mrs. Franklin P. Adams and Mrs. Chotzinoff. Standing: Russel Crouse, Corey Ford, Clifford Spiller, S. Chotzinoff and Frank Sullivan.

PROHIBITION IS DEAD.—Nearly fourteen years of prohibition ended when Utah ratified repeal at 5:32½ P. M.—*Stories p. 3; other pics. pp. 30, 31.*

Liquor from incoming steamers is examined at Appraiser's Office, 201 Varick St., by F. L. Van Etten (left), examiner and his assistants. Every shipment is first tested here. (NEWS photo)

98

"You've forgotten those June nights at the Riviera…. the night I drank Champagne from your slipper – two quarts. It would have been more but you were wearing inner soles."

Groucho Marx, *At the Circus*, 1939

One of the most extensive wine cellars in the world sits
beneath La Tour d'Argent, an historic and celebrated
Paris restaurant. Some 450,000 bottles of wines and spirits dating back more than two centuries sit in the dark
corners of what La Tour d'Argent restaurant calls its
"technically perfect" cellar.

The bottles were saved from the German occupation
during World War Two by Claude Terrail, whose family
still owns the restaurant. He personally walled off part of
the cellars on the night of 14th June 1940 – the day the
Germans entered Paris.

The collection includes a cognac from 1788, the year
before the French Revolution, and a bottle of Champagne
from the first shipment to break through the British
blockade of the American States in 1815.

*"How ironic that Champagne —
long associated with sin and luxury —
should have been invented by a blind
monk."*

Randolph Phillmore

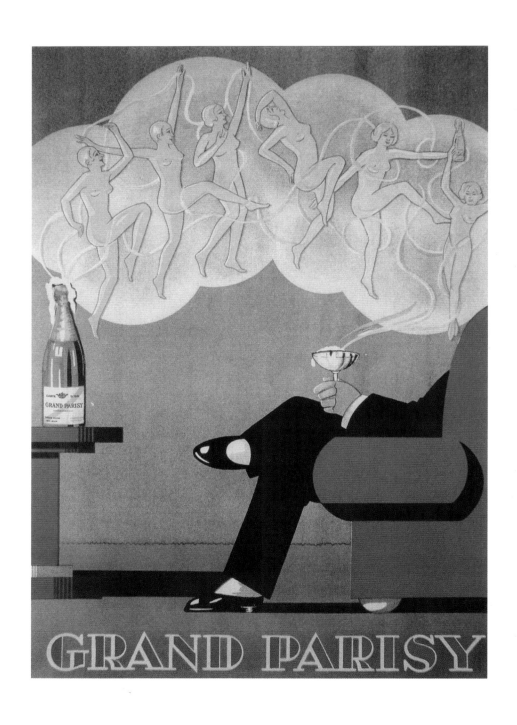

Rick gets the glasses and a bottle of Champagne while Sam starts playing *As Time Goes By.* Rick pours the Champagne and says "Henri wants us to finish the bottle and then three more....

....Here's looking at you, kid.".

PREVIOUS AND THIS PAGE: From *Casablanca*, 1942. Screenplay: Julius J Epstein, Philip G Epstein, Howard Koch.

CHRISTENING THE *USS FRANK KNOX*

– 17th September, 1944

Representing the US Navy and using the traditional bottle of Champagne, sponsor Mrs Annie Reid Knox named this destroyer in honour of her late husband, Frank Knox, Secretary of the US Navy in World War Two between 1940 and his death in April 1944.

The *USS Frank Knox* was built at the Bath Iron Works in Bath, Maine, the first of the Gearing class destroyers. With a speed of 34 knots, its primary object was to provide early warning of air raids to fast carrier task forces in the Western Pacific war zone. On 2nd September 1945 the ship was present in Tokyo Bay when the Japanese surrendered. The *USS Frank Knox* was decommissioned and transferred to the Greek Navy in 1971 and, on 12th September 2001, the old ship was sunk when it was used as a torpedo target by the Greek submarine *Nereus*.

"Here's to Champagne, the drink divine,
that makes us forget all our troubles.
It's made of a dollar's worth of wine,
and three dollars worth of bubbles."
Anonymous

The outbreak of WW2 halted the production of Champagne. Following the invasion and heavy looting, a Führer of Champagne was appointed with a regulatory body in Reims to control production solely for German demands. Some 300,000 to 400,000 bottles of Champagne were dispatched each week to German armed forces on all fronts with priority given to the Luftwaffe and the Deutsche Marine. This inferior Champagne was often sabotaged and made undrinkable whilst the best Champagne was walled up in the extensive cellars and tunnels below Epernay and Reims. In 1941 a new office representing the interests of the Champagne makers was set up in Epernay called the Comité Interprofessionel du Vin de Champagne (CIVC) with the Comte Robert-Jean de Vögué as its chief. A few concessions were extracted from the Führer such as permission to sell a quarter of the annual production to civilians in France, Belgium, Sweden and Finland.

RIGHT: *The bottles have been stamped with identical red labels in German and French which read: 'Wehrmachts - Marketenderware Verkauf in Freien Handel verboten' (Sales in the Free Market are Prohibited) and, 'Reserve a la Wehrmacht, Achat et Revente interdits' (Reserved for German Military Not for Resale or Purchase).*

REIMS CATHEDRAL

On 7th May 1945, Colonel HC Nolen informed the citizens of Reims of Germany's surrender. General Dwight D Eisenhower received 72 bottles of Champagne Pommery 1934 vintage to celebrate France's Liberation and the Signing of the Surrender on 9th May.

The fortnight at Venice passed quickly and sweetly – perhaps too sweetly; I was drowning in honey, stingless. On some days life kept pace with the gondola, as we nosed through the side canals and the boatman uttered his plaintive musical bird-cry of warning; on other days with the speed-boat bouncing over the lagoon in a stream of sun-lit foam; it left a confused memory of fierce sunlight on the sands and cool, marble interiors; of water everywhere, lapping on smooth stone, reflected in a dapple of light on painted ceilings; of a night at the Corombona palace such as Byron might have known, and another Byronic night fishing for scampi in the shallows of Chioggia, the phosphorescent wake of the little ship, the lantern

*swinging in the prow and the net coming up full of weed and
sand and floundering fishes; of melon and prosciutto on the
balcony in the cool of the morning; of hot cheese sandwiches
and Champagne cocktails at Harry's bar.*

Brideshead Revisited, Evelyn Waugh, Chapman & Hall, 1945

Respecting champagne

From B. E. Caulton

Sir, Am I alone in deploring this childish habit of Grand Prix racing drivers (and now even winners of cricket matches) of shaking up their bottles of champagne so that half the contents spew out over all and sundry? Presumably these vandals are all beer drinkers.

Yours faithfully,
B. E. CAULTON,
Willow Brook,
Hedge Lane,
Pylle,
Shepton Mallet,
Somerset.

The Times, Tuesday, 23rd August, 1977

GRAND PRIX

The custom of winning Formula 1 drivers spraying each other with a Jeroboam of Champagne began by accident after a bottle burst open at Le Mans in 1966. Mumm Cordon Rouge is the official Champagne of the 20-race global Formula 1 season.

A Champagne "Christening" is a tradition in the family of
Claude Fourmon, Epernay wine grandee. The seven-week-
old son is held during the ceremony by his mother, who
also bears one of the greatest names in Champagne:
Perrier.

125

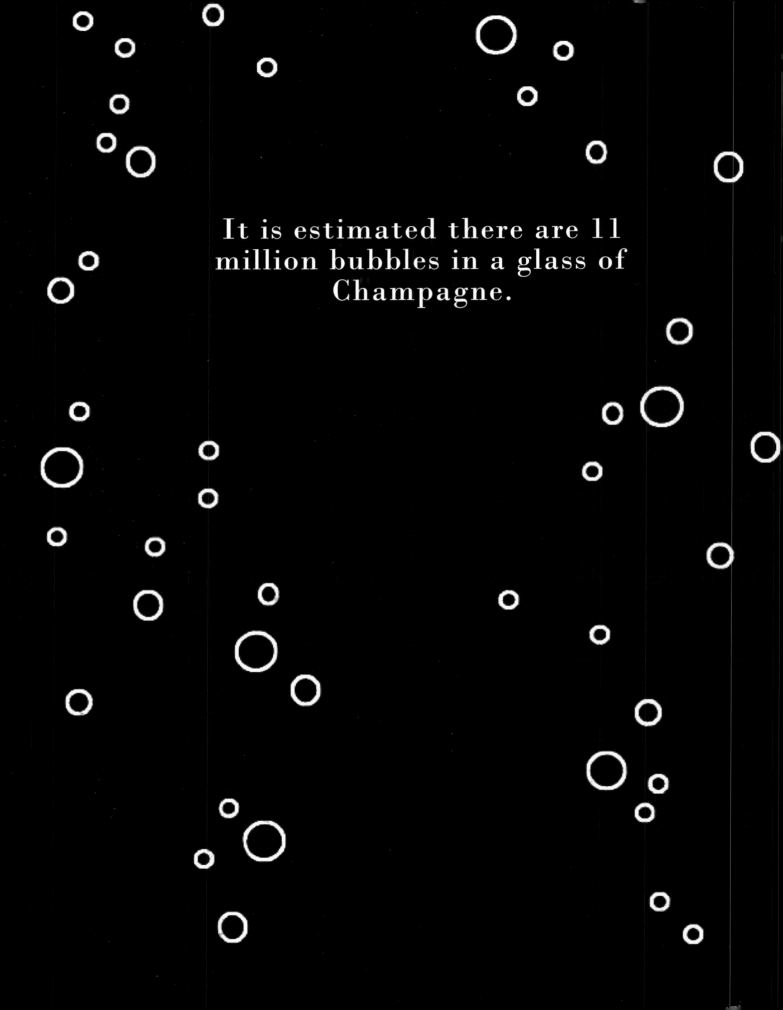

It is estimated there are 11 million bubbles in a glass of Champagne.

*"Why do I drink Champagne for breakfast?
Doesn't everyone?"*

Attributed to Noel Coward

LEFT: *Noel Coward with Jean Claude Pascal and Gisele Preville at the Sarah Bernhardt Theatre, 1952.*

"Hey, did you ever try dunking a potato chip in Champagne? It's real crazy!"

Marilyn Monroe, *The Seven Year Itch*, 1955

As the elegent bachelor Louis Jourdan waltzes Hermione Gingold around the room the young Leslie Caron celebrates *The Night They Invented Champagne.*

The Night They Invented Champagne, Gigi, 1958. Lyrics by Alan Jay Lerner and music by Frederick Loewe

CONSTANTIN SILVESTRI

During a rehearsal in the 1960s, the Rumanian conductor, Constantin Silvestri, said to members of the Bournemouth Symphony Orchestra,

"I shall tell you what are the three best things in life. The first is a glass of Champagne, the third is a cigarette."

Constantin Silvestri

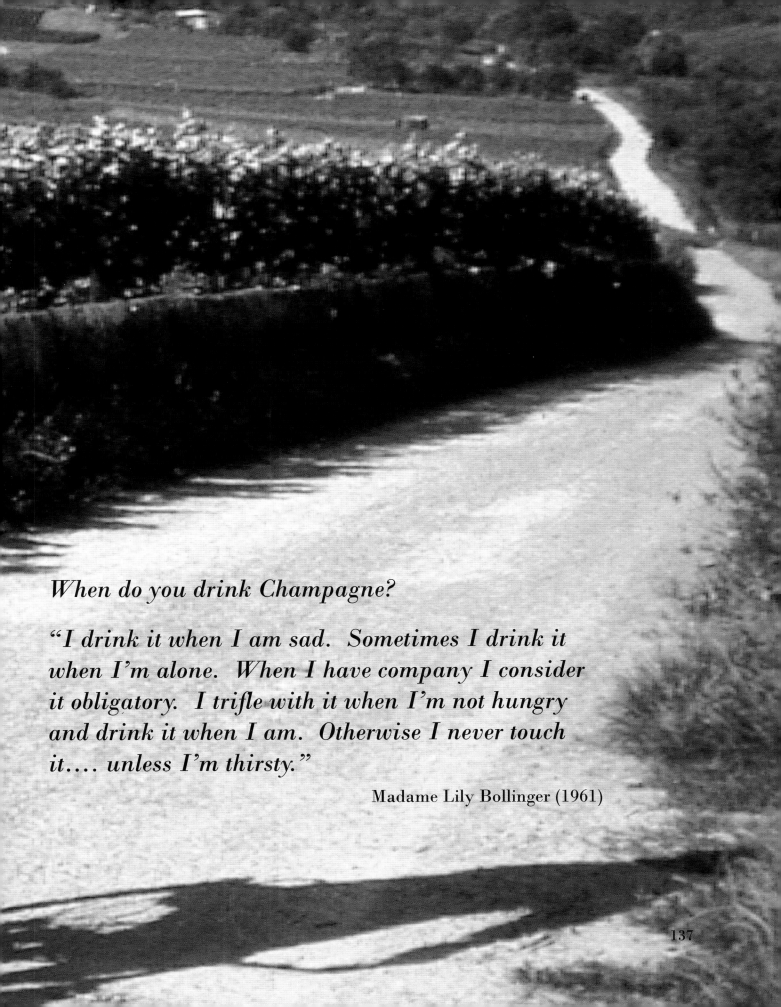

When do you drink Champagne?

"I drink it when I am sad. Sometimes I drink it when I'm alone. When I have company I consider it obligatory. I trifle with it when I'm not hungry and drink it when I am. Otherwise I never touch it…. unless I'm thirsty."

Madame Lily Bollinger (1961)

137

Whitehall quadruples order for champagne

Coalition ministers and senior civil servants were supplied with nearly four times as much champagne last year as the year before, documents show.

Whitehall ordered 204 bottles of champagne in 2013, compared with 53 in 2012, according to papers disclosed under the Freedom of Information Act.

Demand for sparkling wine more than tripled, with orders for 1,236 bottles last year and 360 the year before.

As well as its champagne order, Whitehall consumed 252 bottles of it, including two of Louis Roederer 2000 worth £490 each. The most popular was a non-vintage Heidsieck Heritage Brut, of which officials drank 50 bottles, each worth £30. According to the documents, the government's hospitality wing says that an "exceptional number of national celebrations", such as the Queen's diamond jubilee and the Olympics, resulted in an increased amount of drink.

Tom Payne and Rajeev Syal

"The House of Lords is like a glass of Champagne that has stood for five days."

Clement Attlee

"There comes a time in every woman's life when the only thing that helps is a glass of Champagne."

Bette Davis

TAITTINGER

A party was held to celebrate the 80th birthday of a matriarch of the Taittinger family. To toast her health, a magnum bottle of 80-year-old Taittinger Champagne was produced from their cellars. The head of the family, Claude Taittinger, eased out the cork, poured a little into a glass, appraised the colour and bubbles, sniffed the bouquet, to a sip and announced:

"I am pleased that Madame has aged far better than our Champagne."

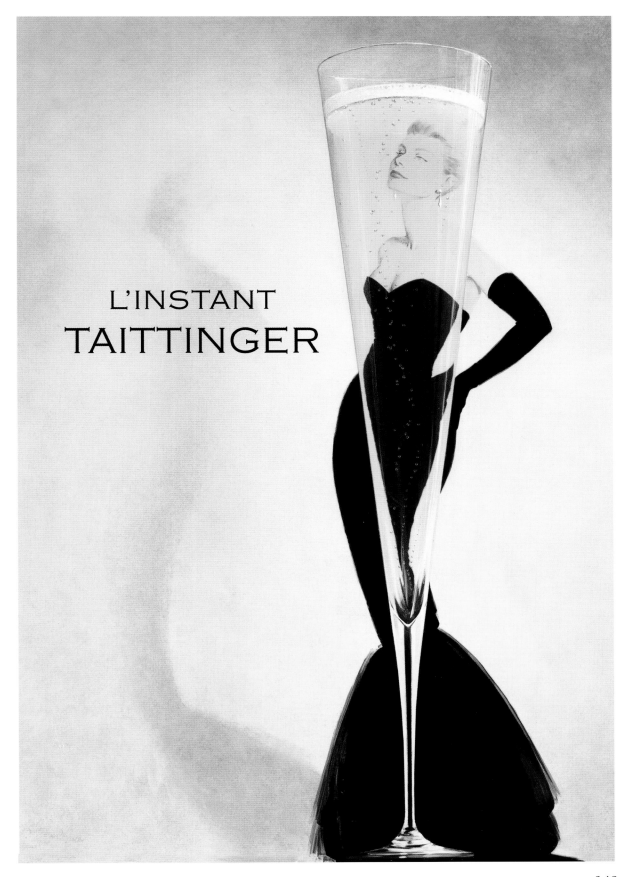

BUBBLE BATHS

Broadway producer Florenz Ziegfeld's estranged wife - the French musical and screen star Anna Held, who gained an outrageous reputation - was one of the celebrity residents at San Francisco's St Francis Hotel. Before she had even crossed the Atlantic to win the hearts of American theatregoers, Miss Held had become famous for taking milk baths. The fetish required thirty gallons of pasteurized milk to be delivered to her hotel suite daily. She once confessed that she preferred something more bubbly. "The milk baths are for publicity," she purred. "Champagne is strictly reserved for pleasure."

A similar sentiment was voiced in more recent times by Katie, a 'Page three Girl' for London's *Sun*, and her male counterpart, Rhydian Lewis. They had been hired by the notorious London tabloid to dip into a bathtub filled with 36 bottles of bubbly at the Portobello Hotel. In 1998 *The Independent* reported that two more guests of the hotel (rumoured to be Kate Moss and actor Johnny Depp) had tried it, but when they had gone for dinner the chambermaid went into the room and pulled out the plug, allowing £750 of Mumm Champagne to drain away. Although filling a bath with three cases of Champagne is a service the hotel routinely offers, it appears that the maid was unaware of it.

Unlike Miss Moss (who refused to comment on the matter) the buxom Katie remarked to reporters: "It's chilly, but oh so sexy. The bubbles get everywhere - and I mean everywhere!"

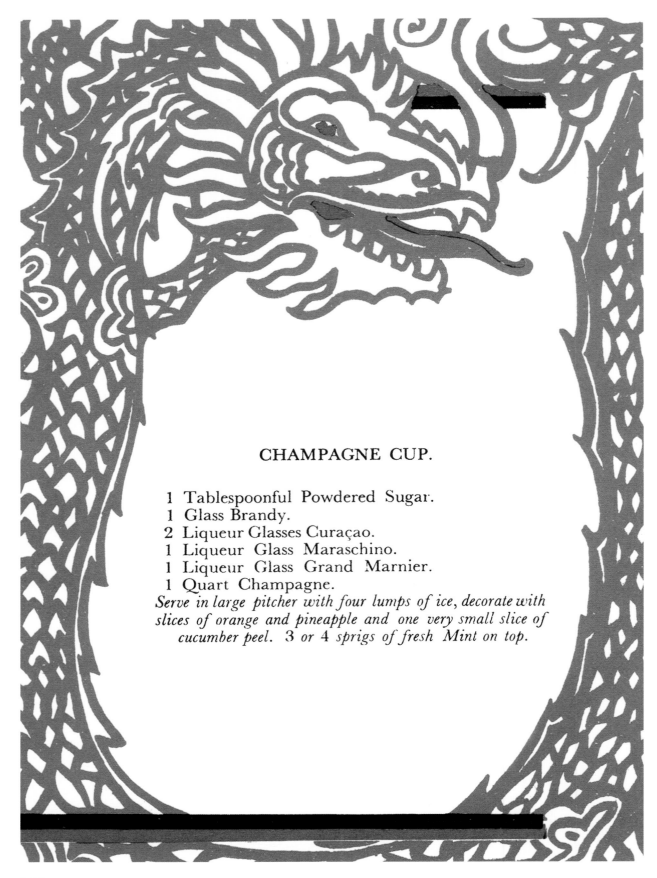

CHAMPAGNE CUP.

1 Tablespoonful Powdered Sugar.
1 Glass Brandy.
2 Liqueur Glasses Curaçao.
1 Liqueur Glass Maraschino.
1 Liqueur Glass Grand Marnier.
1 Quart Champagne.

Serve in large pitcher with four lumps of ice, decorate with slices of orange and pineapple and one very small slice of cucumber peel. 3 or 4 sprigs of fresh Mint on top.

Photograph of a sign board in Carnaby Street, London, W1

JOHN BETJEMAN ON DESERT ISLAND DISCS
with Roy Plomley (12th April 1975)

Roy Plomley: *And one luxury?*

John Betjeman: *A half bottle of Champagne*
                      every morning after breakfast.

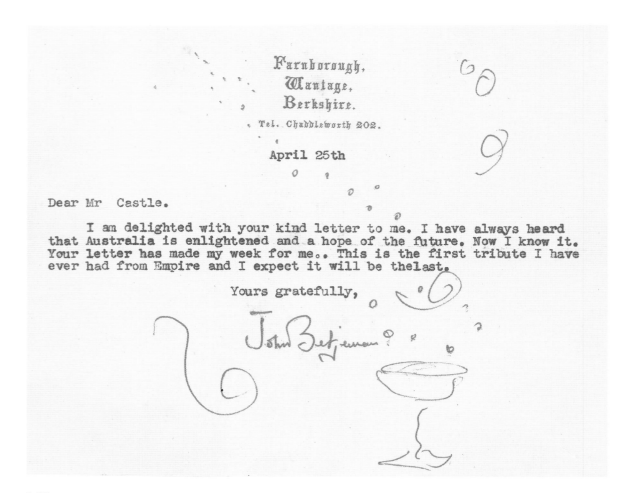

Farnborough,
Wantage,
Berkshire.

Tel. Chaddleworth 202.

April 25th

Dear Mr Castle.

     I am delighted with your kind letter to me. I have always heard
that Australia is enlightened and a hope of the future. Now I know it.
Your letter has made my week for me.. This is the first tribute I have
ever had from Empire and I expect it will be thelast.

     Yours gratefully,

John Betjeman

GLYNDEBOURNE

ORLOFSKY

I sing to the king fermented, tra la la,
Bubbly ornamented, tra la la.
There's simply no describing
The pleasures of imbibing.
The curse of human dryness
Is banished by his highness:
Champagne the first,
The king by acclimation,
The monarch of libation
In bubbly coronation!

ALL

A toast, a toast, a toast!

ORLOFSKY

Then up with a magnum, let it pass,
Rim to rim, glass to glass,
Hail to his spirit, cheer it on,
And drink till the night is gone!

EISENSTEIN

A monk in a monastery, tra la la,
Sings to the golden berry, tra la la.
It makes the life monastic
No longer feel so drastic.
He finds it more consoling
Than even holy rolling.
Champagne the first, &c.

ADELE

In love the effect is awesome, tra la la,
Up like a budding blossom, tra la la.
It makes the heart grow fonder,
Makes blondes look even blonder,
It turns the cold and stony
To thoughts of matrimony!
Champagne the first, &c.

Die Fledermaus, Johann Strauss II

JÖNKÖPING SCHOONER

In the early hours of 3rd November 1916, the Swedish schooner *Jönköping* was sunk by a German U22 submarine off the coast of Finland in the Baltic Sea. The wooden schooner lay at the bottom of the sea at a depth of 64 metres for 80 years until salvagers located the wreck in 1997. Part of its cargo included 50 boxes of Champagne each containing around 100 bottles that were probably intended for the Tsar's imperial court in Russia. A few bottles were brought up to the surface. The labels and the wires had long gone but when the corks were popped they were clearly marked Heidsieck & Co Reims on the bottom and Champagne Goût Américain 1907 on the side. The Champagne was declared excellent. The cellar of the dark, cold sea appeared to have preserved the Champagne while the corks had been held securely in place by the water pressure.

The following year the schooner was partially raised to the surface and more of its cargo of wines and Champagne removed. It had been hoped to restore the ship but it was too damaged to raise completely and so was left to sink back into the sea.

That autumn on 22nd October, Christie's in South Kensington, London, held a Champagne sale which included 24 bottles of the 1907 vintage Heidsieck & Co Monopole Goût Américain discovered in the wreck of the *Jönköping*. The bottles, which had been rewired and sealed in wax, were expected to sell for around £500 each.

On the morning, lots 383 to 406 of the Baltic bubbly sold for up to £2,420 each, well over the estimated price.

"The whole sensation is one of immaculate flavours in complete harmony, and the mousse rises so quickly to the top of the flute that you have to be careful when pouring it. If you want to smell the depths of the Baltic just lift a section of the wax and sniff the cork, but if the successful bidder's bottle is anything like the one I tasted, there will not be even the hint of sea in either its smell or taste, and I have yet to hear of one bottle that deviates from this."

Christie's catalogue

153

RONALD SEARLE ON DESERT ISLAND DISCS
with Sue Lawley (2005)

Sue Lawley:
"And your luxury?"

Ronald Searle:
*"Oh Champagne. I would have
the best possible bottle of Champagne, probably Cristal
Roederer, then I would write a note, put it into the bottle,
throw it into the sea, saying, please send another one."*

The music Searle chose to save from the waves was *The Champagne Song* from *Die Fledermaus*.

"Possibly, because of the peculiarly British pursuit of standing around in damp marquees for several hours at wedding receptions, where the rasping acidity of a young Champagne plays havoc with the stomach, the British consumer has developed a preference for Champagne with

more age, a taste known by some in-
credulous Frenchmen as 'Le Goût
Anglais'."
Christopher Burr, *Christie's International*
Magazine, Oct 1998

THE WORLD'S OLDEST CHAMPAGNE

In 2010 divers found 145 bottles of Champagne and five bottles of beer in a shipwreck south of Föglö, which is in Åland's Finnish-controlled outer archipelago. Once the news that "the world's oldest Champagne had been found in Åland" got out, a media frenzy ensued. Because journalists around the world drew attention to the find, the Åland Provincial Government quickly instigated restrictions on diving in the area to protect the wreck and its contents.

The first bottle retrieved from the depths was found to contain well-preserved, high-class Champagne. Storage conditions – a constant temperature between four and six degrees, the dark surroundings and the pressure both inside the bottles and at the sea bed – had been ideal in ensuring that no salt water could penetrate.

The following year at an auction in Mariehamn, the capital of Åland, the Juglar bottle was sold for 24,000 euros while the Veuve Clicquot Champagne, dating back to approximately 1841, went for 30,000 euros (£26,700), setting a new world record.

The shipwrecked Champagne is not the most expensive ever sold, but it is the most expensive ever auctioned. Compono said the Ritz-Carlton in Moscow offers a bottle of vintage 1907 Heidsieck for $275,000 dollars.

Subsequent marine-archaeological investigations of the ship indicate that she dates from the first half of the 19th century, but her name and origin remain a mystery.

POL ROGER

Once again Champagne Pol Roger gave its support to the annual charity race day at York Race Course.

Jacqueline Coward, grand-daughter of trainer Mick East-erby, won the Queen Mother's Cup riding Crackentorp at odds of 8-1.

As tradition demanded the jockey received her weight in Pol Roger Champagne which, on this occasion, consisted of five cases and one bottle, a total of 31 bottles, all of which was loaded on to the antique scales in the winner's enclosure.

Source: *The York Press*, June 2011

"I was never drunk. True, I was drinking five bottles of Champagne a day (during the filming of the original series of Dallas), but I was never drunk. I just took little slugs throughout the day. Nine o'clock in the morning to nine o'clock at night is 12 long hours. You can ingest a lot of alcohol in that time, but it was never too much."

Larry Hagman, *Independent on Sunday*, 2nd Sept 2012

"Jockeys drink Champagne as an everyday tipple, since it goes to the head without thickening the waist."

Clive James, *Encounter*, November 1975

ROYAL ASCOT 2013

Races: 30

Prize money: Five million

Spectators: 280,000

Food: Total of 2,050 kg of fresh lobster, 35,000 asparagus spears and 30,000 chocolate eclairs eaten during the week

Drink: Estimated 170,000 pints of beer and 50,000 bottles of Champagne consumed

POP CHAMPAGNE

all the girls give it to me
i aint gotta take it

oh
pop champagne ohh
pop champagne ohh
we pop champagne ohh
we pop champagne

we need more bottles tell ma hurry up
tell em Ron Browz here, hottest in America
gimme 16 bars and u know ill tear it up
know its me when u see the spur in ya area
and she call me all night cause you cant get it up
on my neck on my wrist
everything is blitted up
drinkin bottles of that clique till I spit it up
only gettin one life so u gotta live it up

if you in the things im in
shawty we can be friends
shawty we can be friends
but right now

I wanna see you dance see you dance
I wanna see you dance see you dance
I wanna see you dance see you dance
I wanna see you dance see you dance

HENLEY ROYAL REGATTA

Henley Royal Regatta is undoubtedly the best known
regatta in the world and is both one of the highlights of
the summer sporting calendar and the social season.

It attracts thousands of visitors over a five-day period and spectators will be thrilled by over 200 races of an international standard, including Olympians and crews new to the event.

"Champagne is by its very nature a celebratory drink and one to be enjoyed with loved ones.

I started saving Champagne corks when I graduated from University. The night before I left for home, I sat with some friends on top of the removal van that loaded all my belongings drinking Champagne straight from the bottle.

It was a moment I wanted to preserve, so I placed the cork in a bowl as a keepsake. It was soon joined by more corks from birthdays, anniversaries, weddings, holidays, dinners with family and friends, and many other occasions worthy of celebration.

At this point, I have no idea which cork is associated with each moment, and as time passes, I can't say that I remember every event. But it is a collection of happy times and a reminder of how fortunate I am.

I now realize that the bowl itself is worth celebrating, so I will put down my pen and pick up a glass."

Brett Brubaker

HONEY MONEY

The Conservative Party's Summer Fundraising Ball was held at the Hurlingham Club, Fulham, west London on 2nd July 2014.

The extraordinary prize of playing tennis with David Cameron and Boris Johnson was the star lot at the Conservative Party's Summer Fundraising Ball on Wednesday 2nd July 2014. It was billed as giving the successful bidder the chance to play "the ultimate tennis match" and was sold off by the Conservative Party for £160,000 to the banker wife of a former minister in Vladimir Putin's government. The auction winner was Lubov Chernukhin, the wife of Vladimir Chernuhkin, who was Russian's deputy finance minister during Putin's first term in office.

A bottle of Champagne signed by Margaret Thatcher sold for £45,000. Other prizes at the auction included a "fantastic eight-gun pheasant shoot" at Tusmore, the Oxfordshire estate of the Syrian-born billionaire, Wafic Said, which one guest told The Guardian *sold for £80,000. The source added that the auctioneer, foreign office minister Hugo Swire, put up a jar of honey made by his own bees, saying he wanted it to become the most expensive pot of honey ever sold. It went for £15,000, the source said.*

The Guardian, Friday, 4th July 2014

"Gentlemen, in the little moment that remains to us between the crisis and the catastrophe, we may as well drink a glass of Champagne."

Paul Claudel

CREDITS

Endpapers: © Brett Brubaker; p. 2: The Art Archive/Culver Pictures; p. 6: © BBC Photo Library; pp. 12-25: © Michel Jolyot; p. 33: illustration reproduced with permission from the Mary Petty and Alan Dunn Estate at Syracuse University, Syracuse, NY, USA; p. 40: photo © Michèle Clément-Delbos; p. 41: © Victoria & Albert Museum, London; pp. 42-43: Library of Congress Prints & Photographs Division, Washington D.C.; pp. 45, 46-47: © Grenna Museum, Gränna, Sweden; p. 49: © Roger-Viollet/Getty Images; pp. 52-53: © Michel Dubré; p. 54: image from Décors de Bordels by Nicole Canet, 2011/© Galérie au Bonheur du Jour, Paris; p. 56: © Collection Moët & Chandon; pp. 58-59: reproduced from Jean-Baptiste Charcot, Explorateur des mers, navigateur des poles, © 2006 Editions Glénat; p. 61 - Scott Polar Research Institute, University of Cambridge; pp. 62-63: photograph by Edward Nelson/Private Collection/Christies Images/Bridgeman Images; p. 63: pen and body-colour on card by Edward Nelson/Private Collection/Christies Images/Bridgeman Images; pp. 64-65: reproduced with permission from *The Savoy Cocktail Book*, 1930; pp. 70, 71: 1911 photograph © Dover Museum; p. 74: © National Museums Northern Ireland, Collection Ulster Folk & Transport Museum; p. 79: © Bettmann/CORBIS; p. 81: courtesy of Captain Pandapants via Flickr; p. 84: © Roger-Viollet/Getty Images; p. 85: illustration by Lou Mayer, © Illustrated London News/Mary Evans; p. 86: photo © Michèle Clément-Delbos; p. 89: Isadora Duncan Dance Foundation (Lori Belilove, Artistic Director, pictured as Isadora Duncan); p. 97: © Stanley Greenberg/Esto; p. 98 (above): photo by NY Daily News via Getty Images; p. 98 (below): reproduced with permission from *The Savoy Cocktail Book*, 1930; p. 99: The Art Archive/Collection Dagli Orti; p. 100: © MPI/Getty Images; pp. 102, 103: La Tour d'Argent, Paris; pp. 105, 106-7: © Warner Bros/The Kobal Collection/Jack Woods; pp. 108, 109: Naval History & Heritage Command, Washington D.C.; p. 112: Musée Calvet, Avignon; p. 115: © Paul Tonge; p. 128: © Keystone/Getty Images; pp. 131, 133: Ronald Grant Archive; pp. 136-7: Champagne Bollinger; p. 141: 20th Century Fox/The Kobal Collection; p. 143: © Champagne Taittinger; pp. 144-5: © Bettman/CORBIS; p. 146: reproduced with permission from *The Savoy Cocktail Book*, 1930; p. 147: photo © Michèle Clément-Delbos; p. 148: © John Betjeman, by permission of the John Betjeman Estate; p. 149: © Topfoto; p. 156: reproduced with kind permission of Kate Searle; p. 157: reproduced with permission of

ACKNOWLEDGEMENTS

Without the help of these people this book would not
have been possible:

Cathie Arrington,
Chris Beetles,
Michèle Clément-Delbos,
Kate and Ian Craig,
Rose Foot,
David Ford,
Léonard Lassalle,
Joanna Lumley,
Francoise Peretti,
William Salaman,
Jancis Robinson,
Selina Skipwith,
Jason Yapp

and my wife Helen.

First published in Great Britain by LochAwe Books in 2015

Copyright © John Burningham
ISBN 978-0-9933862-0-6

Printed and bound in Latvia by Livonia

184